D1060681

A Taste Of The World
What People Eat and How They Celebrate Around the World

Illustrated & Written by Beth Walrond

This book was edited and designed by gestalten.

Edited by Robert Klanten and Angela Sangma Francis

Design and Layout by Constanze Hein, Book Book

Typeface: Basis Grotesque by Colophon Foundry,
Malaussène Translation by Laure Afchain

Printed by Schleunungdruck GmbH, Marktheidenfeld
Made in Germany

Published by Little Gestalten, Berlin 2019
ISBN 978-3-89955-818-0

2nd printing, 2019

© Die Gestalten Verlag GmbH & Co. KG, Berlin 2019

Thank you to my mum and dad, for all their support and love.
To Ed, for all the tasty food, and to all my friends around the world
for all their inspiration and advice.

All rights reserved. No part of this publication may be reproduced
or transmitted in any form or by any means, electronic or mechanical,
including photocopy or any storage and retrieval system, without
permission in writing from the publisher.

Respect copyrights, encourage creativity!

For more information, and to order books, please visit
www.little.gestalten.com.

Bibliographic information published by the Deutsche Nationalbibliothek.
The Deutsche Nationalbibliothek lists this publication in the Deutsche
Nationalbibliografie; detailed bibliographic data are available online
at www.dnb.de.

This book was printed on paper certified according to the
standards of the FSC®.

FSC
www.fsc.org

MIX
Paper from
responsible sources
FSC® C105039

A TASTE OF THE WORLD

What People Eat and How They Celebrate Around the Globe

LITTLE GESTALTEN

FOOD IS ALL ABOUT SHARING

This book shows how people around the world come together to cook and eat all kinds of meals, from a tasty everyday breakfast to a delicious festival feast. Every dish has a special place in the country to which it belongs and is special to those who make it.

Get ready to go on a journey to find out what makes each country's food so special. Discover new and exciting ingredients and dishes from different places.

Find out how people around the world celebrate with food at over 20 festivals. Customs and traditions about food can be hundreds and sometimes even thousands of years old.

A Taste of the World is a celebration of how different cultures use food every day and to honor special occasions and come together.

IT BRINGS PEOPLE TOGETHER

ASIA & THE MIDDLE EAST

Turkey

Iran

India

Bay of

Indian
Ocean

Rice is the seed that grows on a certain type of grass. It was first grown in ancient southern China but it is now grown all over the world.

Long, medium, and short grain are the three main types of rice. It can be white, yellow, golden, brown, purple, red, or black.

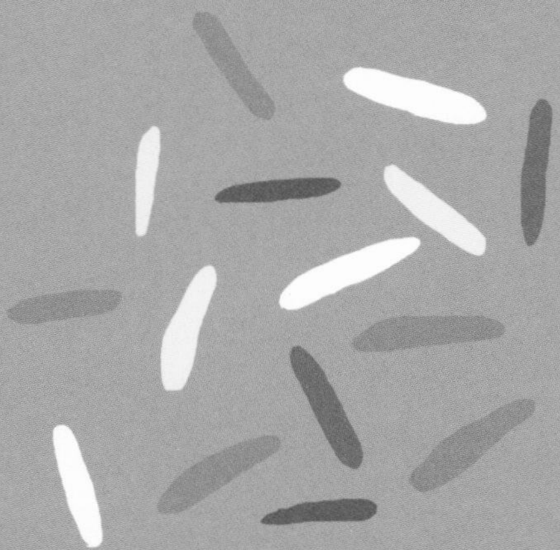

long brown

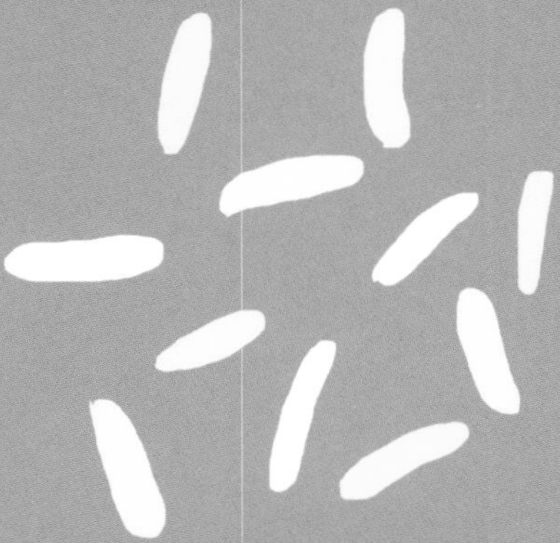

basmati

sushi

RICE

arborio or risotto

wild

jasmine

6

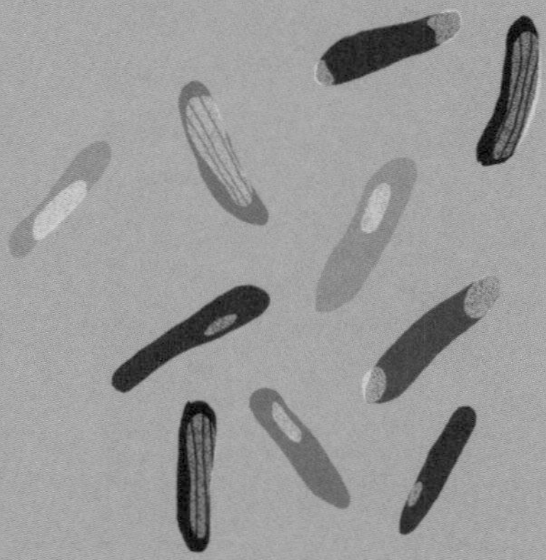

How is rice grown?

1. Plough: First the ground is ploughed and made ready for the seedlings.

2. Plant: The seedlings are planted in neat rows. The paddy fields are kept full of water.

3. Grow: After a flower appears, a tiny grain grows. The outer layer of the grain is called a husk. It is like a protective jacket.

Rice is grown in paddy fields, which are fields that are flooded with water. There are low walls around the outside to keep the water in.

4. Harvest: In late summer, the rice is harvested. The rice plants are bundled together and left to dry in the sun.

5. Thresh: Next the rice grains are separated from the stalks, usually by hitting them against a hard surface.

6. Winnow: Now the edible rice grains are separated from the inedible husks. Everything is tossed in woven trays or baskets. The heavy edible rice grains collect in the tray, while the light inedible husks blow away in the wind.

CHINA

Ancient Chinese history is divided into dynasties. Each dynasty marks a time when a particular line of emperors ruled. Around 600 years ago, during the Ming dynasty, part of the Great Wall of China was built with a paste made from sticky rice flour. Sticky rice mortar was one of the greatest inventions of the time. It was used to build tombs and walls that stayed in place even during earthquakes.

Around 5,000 years ago, chopsticks were invented in China. At first chopsticks were used to cook with rather than for eating, but everyone quickly realized they were the perfect way to eat noodles. Soon chopsticks became popular in countries across Asia.

Dim sum are small dishes of bite sized food.

It's said, the longer the noodle, the longer your life. This calls for a lot of slurping!

rice noodle rolls

dumplings

steamed buns

These foods are said to bring about good wishes:

whole fish for togetherness

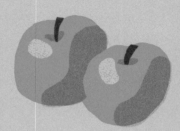

apples for peace

sweet rice cakes for a prosperous year ahead

8

At New Year people gather in their homes to prepare feasts. In an ancient Chinese legend, a ferocious horned monster, called Nian, lives at the bottom of the sea. On New Year's Eve Nian comes ashore to hunt. Today there is still the custom of making offerings of food to Nian. People also set off firecrackers to scare him away.

XIN NIAN
Chinese New Year

Chinese New Year marks the beginning of a new year on the traditional Chinese calendar. Each year the date changes, but celebrations always begin on the first new moon that appears between January 21 and February 20. Celebrations for Chinese New Year last for 15 days. There are many big parties and parades in the streets.

INDIA

Indian cuisine is often a mix of regional and traditional dishes, with many using locally available herbs, vegetables, fruits and spices.

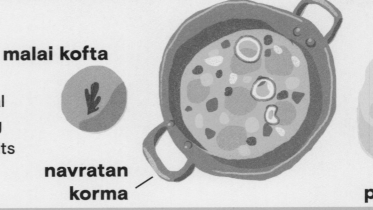

malai kofta

navratan korma

poori

Masala is a special mixture of spices that gives the base flavor to an Indian dish. A masala can be a ground powder or a paste. In India, there are many different kinds of masala.

masala

chai

Chai masala is a sweet, hot, spicy, milky tea. The masala is made with green cardamom pods, cinnamon sticks, ground cloves, ground ginger, and black peppercorns.

Snacks and treats are eaten all over India

lassi

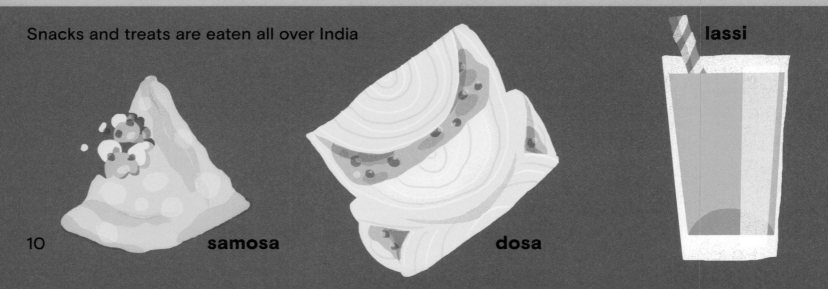

samosa

dosa

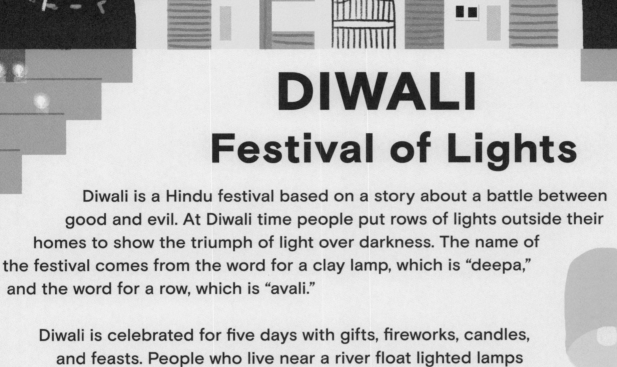

DIWALI
Festival of Lights

Diwali is a Hindu festival based on a story about a battle between good and evil. At Diwali time people put rows of lights outside their homes to show the triumph of light over darkness. The name of the festival comes from the word for a clay lamp, which is "deepa," and the word for a row, which is "avali."

Diwali is celebrated for five days with gifts, fireworks, candles, and feasts. People who live near a river float lighted lamps on tiny rafts. Many traditional homemade Diwali dishes are fried in hot, smoking golden oil, which fits perfectly with the theme of the celebration of light.

Over the centuries Diwali has become a national festival that Indians of all religions celebrate.

JAPAN

Japan is a country made up of islands, so there's plenty of fresh fish to eat. One of Japan's most popular dishes is sushi. This dish is made from sticky rice and other ingredients such as seafood or vegetables which are sometimes wrapped in seaweed. Sushi chefs can spend their whole lives learning to perfect the delicate art of making pretty and colorful sushi that is full of interesting flavors.

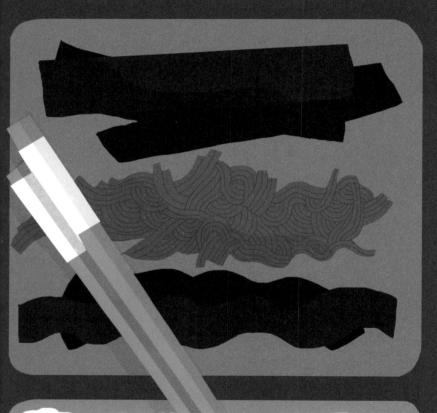

What's bento?

Bento is a decorated box used for a packed lunch. It takes time and care to make the food for a bento box because it can be arranged to look like animals, people, or even cartoon characters.

Five tastes

There are five main tastes: sweet, sour, salty, bitter, and umami. Umami is a Japanese word that means "pleasantly savoury".

Long ago people believed gods lived inside cherry trees. When the trees came into blossom, people gathered underneath to have a party. They blessed the year's harvest, announced the beginning of the rice-planting season, and welcomed spring. This old custom, called Hanami, means "flower viewing," and it still happens today.

HANAMI
Cherry Blossom Festival

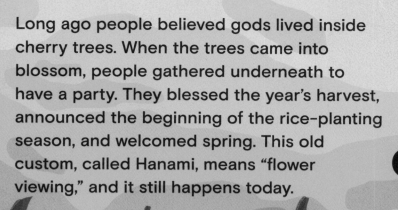

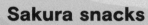

Sakura snacks
Sakura means "cherry blossom." During Hanami, there are many sakura-flavored snacks and drinks.

Onigiri
This is a favorite dish for picnics. Onigiri are rice balls made into interesting shapes.

Mochi
Mochi is a sweet rice cake. Sakura mochi are filled with red bean paste and wrapped in a salted cherry blossom leaf.

THAILAND

In Thailand, almost every dish combines a perfect blend of salty, sweet, spicy and sour flavors.

The sweet flavor and golden color of a mango symbolizes prosperity.

These dishes are eaten at Songkran

poa pee

mango sticky rice

larb gai fortune chicken

egg rolls for wealth and luck

Thai chicken salad for good fortune

SONGKRAN
New Year

Thai New Year is called Songkran. The festival has a fun and happy water theme. To mark the beginning of a brand new year, people celebrate in the streets by firing water pistols and throwing buckets of ice-cold water over each other.

In Thailand, the words for rice and food are the same—"khao". Rice is the first and most important part of any meal. It's eaten for breakfast, lunch, and dinner. The usual Thai greeting "kin khao reu yang?" means, "have you eaten rice yet?"

TURKEY

Turkish cuisine today has been heavily influenced by the food of the Ottoman Empire. This was one of the biggest and longest-lasting empires in history. The sultan's palace in Istanbul could have up to 1,300 staff preparing food for thousands of people. Often roses were used to flavor dishes. Today flowers are still used to flavor ice cream, jam, and Turkish delight.

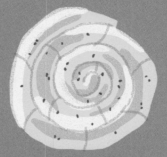

Börek
A börek is a flaky layered pastry filled with meat or cheese. Often it is eaten at breakfast.

Kebab
Turkey's national dish is the kebab, which is meat and vegetables grilled on a skewer.

Yogurt
Long ago herdsmen stored milk in the guts of animals. Soon they discovered that the milk curdled and thickened. The word "yogurt" comes from the Turkish word "yoğurmak", which means to thicken. Ayran is a popular yogurt drink that is sipped slowly during a meal. Nowadays yogurt is eaten all over the world. It can taste salty, tangy, or sweet.

Dolma
Dolma means "stuffed." Meat and vegetables are stuffed into tomatoes, eggplants, and vine leaves.

ŞEKER BAYRAMI
The Sugar Feast

This festival is called the Sugar Feast because people treat each other to sweets and desserts. Celebrations start immediately after Ramadan, which is a period of 30 days when Muslims don't eat or drink in the hours of daylight. On the first day of Sugar Feast, families wake early, dress in their best clothes, and eat a large breakfast together. Later, children go from door to door wishing people a happy "Bayram". In return, they receive sweets and chocolates. The festival lasts for three days.

IRAN

Iran, which used to be
called Persia, is one of the
oldest civilizations in the world.
In Iran, the cuisine has a rich history
which has remained almost unchanged
for centuries.

Fresh and tangy

Iranian cooking contains many sour flavors, including pomegranate,
lemon, and sour orange. Between courses people eat fresh herbs to
keep their mouths fresh for the next dish.

Nuts about nuts

Iran is one of the world's biggest producers
of pistachio nuts. Iranians call the pistachio
"the smiling nut."

The Iranian, or Persian, New Year is called Nowruz. It is celebrated with a table set with seven types of food, which all stand for hope. This is called a Haft-Seen, which means "seven S's," because each food starts with the letter S. There's "somagh", or sumac, "seer", or garlic, "seeb", or apples, "senjed", or dried fruit, "samanu", or sweet wheat germ pudding, "sabzeh", or sprouts, and "serekh", or vinegar. Rosewater and a book of poetry might be placed on the table for luck too.

The old year goes out with a bang. Children run through the streets clanging spoons on pots and pans. The children knock on their neighbors' doors and ask for sweets. This tradition is called Ghashogh-Zani, or "spoon beating."

AFRICA

North
Atlantic
Ocean

Morocco

Nigeria

South
Atlantic
Ocean

Egypt

Ethiopia

Indian
Ocean

What are spices?

Spices are the seeds, fruits, or roots of different plants.
Spices can add heat, exciting flavors, and rich colors to food.
Most spices are grown in tropical parts of the world.

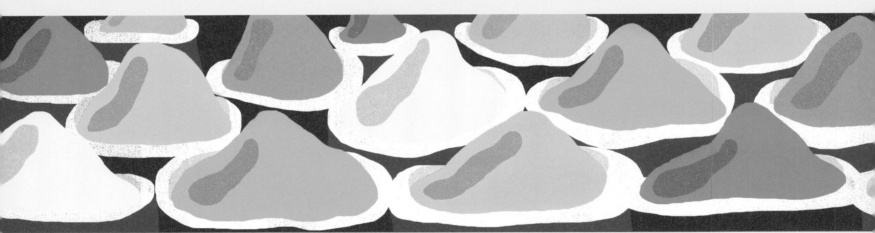

Spice or gold?

Did you know that in medieval Europe nutmeg was more valuable than gold? Today the most expensive and sought after spice in the world is saffron. It is commonly known as red gold.

Spices were once very precious! The quest for spices led to many explorers discovering new lands. When Christopher Columbus set sail across the Atlantic he was looking for pepper.

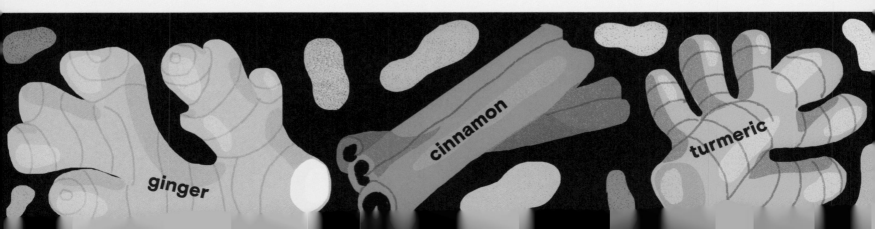

Thousands of years ago, the ancient Egyptians flavored their food with spices. Spices were also used to embalm, or preserve, the ancient Egyptian dead. Before a body was mummified, it was rinsed out with anise and cumin.

SPICES

Many people believe that spices have health-giving properties. If you eat enough pepper, you start to sweat, which in ancient times was thought to be an excellent medical treatment. In the past, spices were also used to disguise the flavor of rotting food, especially meat.

ETHIOPIA

Ethiopian cuisine is known for its thick, spicy meat stews and vegetable side dishes and it is also the birthplace of coffee. The first coffee plants grew here and a common Ethiopian saying is "buna dabo naw," which means "coffee is our bread."

Injera

Injera bread is key to Ethiopian food. It is a spongy flatbread that is torn and used to scoop food into the mouth. It is made out of teff, which is the world's smallest grain. Injera has a pleasantly sour taste. A delicious sweet treat is injera bread wrapped around a fresh slab of honeycomb, sometimes with young honey bee grubs wriggling around inside.

Wat

Wat is an Ethiopian spicy stew, which can be made from meat, vegetables, and spices.

Berbere

Ethiopians use a special spice mix called berbere.

Gursha

"Gursha" is the Ethiopian word for preparing handfuls of food and feeding them to your friends and family. This shows warmth and care.

ENKUTATASH
New Year

The name Enkutatash means "gift of jewels." It is said that when the Queen of Sheba returned from a visit to King Solomon in Jerusalem, she was greeted with gifts of precious stones by the people of her country. Enkutatash is the first day of the Ethiopian new year and is celebrated on September 11. The day marks the approximate end of the rainy season.

It is a time to be thankful for the rain that has helped crops to grow, and to be hopeful for sunny days ahead. When the long spring rains end, the highlands are covered with wildflowers. Children wear brand-new clothes. They dance and give bouquets of flowers and painted pictures to friends and family.

NIGERIA

Kola nut
The kola nut comes from the fruit of the kola tree. It is used to flavor cola drinks and contains caffeine.

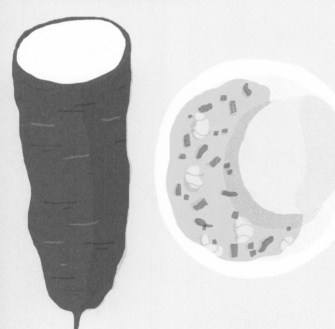

Cassava
Cassava is a starchy root that is pounded to make a paste called fufu. Cassava doesn't taste of much by itself, but it's delicious when made into small balls and dipped into different flavored soups.

Yam
The yam is a tuber that looks like a sweet potato. The Igbo people of southeastern Nigeria celebrate the New Yam Festival, which is held at the end of the rainy season in early August. Hundreds of people come together to say thank you for the yam crop. The oldest man in the village eats the season's first yam.

ARGUNGU
Fish and Cultural Festival

The country Nigeria gets its name from the Niger River, which flows for 2,597 miles (4,180 km) through West Africa. The river provides water to help crops to grow. There are fish to catch and eat. And all kinds of goods are transported up and down its busy waters.

The Argungu Fishing and Cultural Festival is held on the banks of the Matan Fada River. Usually this four-day festival is celebrated in February. Months before the festival, the river is blocked off, trapping fish in one part of the river. When the celebration begins, hundreds of fishermen jump into the river to scare the fish into their nets.

MOROCCO

Couscous

The Berbers were some of the first people to live in Morocco. They farmed crops, such as olives, figs, and dates. The Berbers created a dish, called couscous, which we still eat today. Couscous is made from semolina flour that is spritzed with water and rolled by hand into tiny balls.

ras el hanout

Tagine

"Tagine" is the word for both a stew and the cone-shaped pot it is cooked in. A tagine stew is made by simmering meat with fruits, olives, preserved lemons, and spices. The cone shape of the cooking pot helps trap the steam and keeps the food tender.

Tea time

In Morocco, mint tea is served with every meal. Preparing and pouring mint tea is an art.

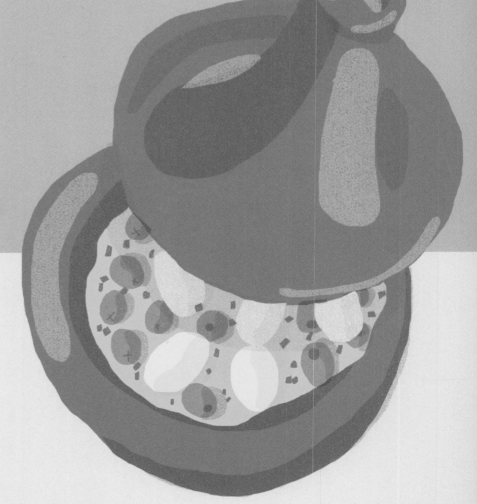

ALMOND BLOSSOM FESTIVAL

Early in February, almond trees on Moroccan mountainsides burst in bloom. Each spring people gather in the town of Tafraoute to celebrate the Almond Blossom Festival. They dance, sing songs, tell traditional stories, drink mint tea, and eat lots of almonds.

Many Moroccan dishes contain sweet nutty almonds.

m`hanncha   **chicken tagine with almonds**   **almond briouat**

EGYPT

Today many Egyptian dishes are very similar to those from ancient times. Ancient Egyptians showed their love of food by painting and carving pictures of huge feasts of meats, fruits, and honey-sweetened cakes on their tombs and temples. Garlic has been found in Egyptian pyramids. It's believed garlic was fed to workers to make them strong and stop them from getting ill.

Each year there are heavy rains and the water in the River Nile rises. Fertile soil spreads along its banks and lush crops can grow. The ancient Egyptians worshipped the god Hapi because they thought he caused the River Nile to flood.

Halva
Halva is a sweet treat made from the paste of sesame seeds. Unlike chocolate it does not melt in the heat.

Aish
Aish is the Arabic name for bread and means "life." Often this kind of bread is used instead of a spoon to scoop up food.

Ful mudammas
This dish of cooked, creamy fava beans was first eaten in ancient times. Today it is often served with a side of aish.

SHAM EL-NESSIM FESTIVAL
Spring Festival

Sham El-Nessim "inhaling the breeze" festival dates back 5,000 years and marks the arrival of spring. On the day of the festival, people wake early and head out to watch the sunrise. They take a picnic of fish, onions, and eggs, which are all traditional festival foods.

Fish

Fesikh is a dish eaten only during the festival. Fish are dried in the sun, then preserved in vats of salt for 45 days. This type of fermented fish dish dates back to pharaonic times, when people saw the waters of the River Nile pull back to leave many rotting fish in its wake.

Onions

In an Egyptian legend, one of the pharaoh's daughters suffered from an incurable disease. Doctors didn't know what to do until a high priest gave her medicine, which was onion juice. She recovered. The pharaoh, her father, was thrilled and declared the day an official celebration in honor of the onion.

EUROPE

Atlantic
Ocean

North
Sea

United
Kingdom

France

Spain

Mediterranean
Sea

Sweden

Germany

Italy

Black
Sea

Grains are the seeds of grasses. Grains are small, hard, and dry, so they are easy to store. When there is spare grain from a harvest, it can be stored to use another time. Many people think that long ago the first grain farmers lived near the land they farmed. Soon settlements and villages began to grow in these places.

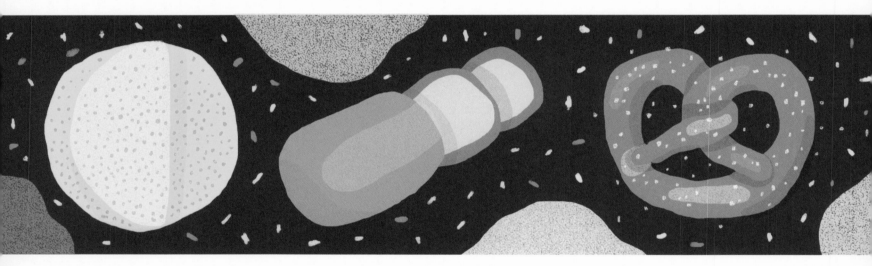

What food do grains make?

Different flours can be used to make many types of food including bread, pasta, oatmeal, tortillas and of course, cake!

GRAINS

wheat

barley

Different grains are grown all over the world and are eaten in almost every culture. Some of the most commonly grown grains are ...

oats

corn

millet

FRANCE

France proudly produces a cheese for every day of the year. And Camembert is a particularly special one that was developed during the French Revolution. The story goes that a local cheesemaker from the town of Camembert once gave shelter to a priest. In return for his help, the priest showed him the secret way to make soft white cheese. Inspired, the cheesemaker made his own, which became known as Camembert.

The word "cuisine" is French.

brie

camembert

The baguette

Once bakers were forbidden by law to start work before 4 am. This meant there was not enough time to cook a loaf for breakfast. What did the bakers do? They baked long thin loaves that cooked more quickly. The baguette was born.

LE 14 JUILLET Bastille Day

On July 14, the national day of France, Bastille Day, is celebrated all over France. On this day in 1789, the people of Paris stormed the Bastille, which was a fortress and prison. Many see this event as the beginning of the French Revolution, when the French people overthrew the king and queen to take back control.

Usually, on the evening before Bastille Day, there are grand balls and parties. Then, on the morning itself, Europe's largest and oldest military parade takes place in Paris. In the afternoon, people celebrate in the street. A simple French Bastille Day picnic might be a fresh baguette, a wheel of cheese, and pâté. The day ends with colorful fireworks lighting up the sky across France.

pâté

quiche

baguette

ITALY

In Italy, the food is known for its delicious simplicity, with many dishes made up of only two to four main ingredients. Pasta is a major part of its cuisine and there are over 450 different pasta shapes and almost as many kinds of sauce. Most pasta is made from durum wheat.

Royal pizza

Pizza was invented in the city of Naples for busy workers. Then, legend has it, Queen Margherita ordered a pizza maker to top flatbread with three toppings in the colors of the Italian flag—white mozzarella cheese, red tomatoes, and green basil. She loved it so much the pizza was named after her, Margherita.

Gelato

Gelato is a type of ice cream. It's made with more milk but less cream and eggs than regular ice cream. It is churned more slowly than ice cream, which means there's less air and the gelato becomes really thick. In southern Italy, gelato is eaten in a sweet brioche bun.

CARNEVALE
Carnival

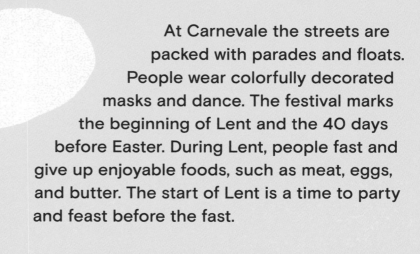

At Carnevale the streets are packed with parades and floats. People wear colorfully decorated masks and dance. The festival marks the beginning of Lent and the 40 days before Easter. During Lent, people fast and give up enjoyable foods, such as meat, eggs, and butter. The start of Lent is a time to party and feast before the fast.

Cities across Italy celebrate Carnevale in different ways. In Ivrea, people throw around 400 tons of oranges in the Battle of the Oranges, then sit down to eat codfish and polenta. In Fano, visitors are showered in sweets. In Verona, a parade is held in honor of Papà del Gnoco, who was a bearded king who loved to eat potato dumplings called gnocchi.

Carpaccio
Raw slices of beef drizzled in olive oil and lemon juice.

SWEDEN

The arctic north of Sweden is called the land of the midnight sun because during the summer the sun never sets.

The Vikings

Once Sweden was the land of Vikings. These seafaring raiders needed food that would last on their long sea voyages. So, over 1,000 years ago, the Scandinavian tradition of smoking and salting food began. Today there are still plenty of cured meats, fish, fruits, and vegetables on a Swedish menu.

Crayfish party

Kräftskiva is a crayfish party. In August on warm summer nights, people eat platefuls of bright red crayfish outside, in gardens and by lakes.

MIDSOMMAR
Midsummer

Midsummer festivities welcome summertime and the growing season. People decorate their houses with green leaves. Some even dress up as "green men" by wrapping themselves in ferns. There's also dancing around a maypole decorated with flowers.

Midsummer is a time to gather with friends. The day begins with picking flowers and making wreaths to wear. There's a custom of young children collecting seven different flowers to put under their pillows before they sleep. The hope is that they dream of their future loves. The midsummer feast is filled with treats, such as pickled herring and boiled new potatoes dressed with fresh dill. Dessert can be the best fresh strawberries served with cream.

SPAIN

Food in Spain is all about making the most of the best local produce. In the south, where the reddest, ripest tomatoes grow, people drink a cold tomato soup called gazpacho.

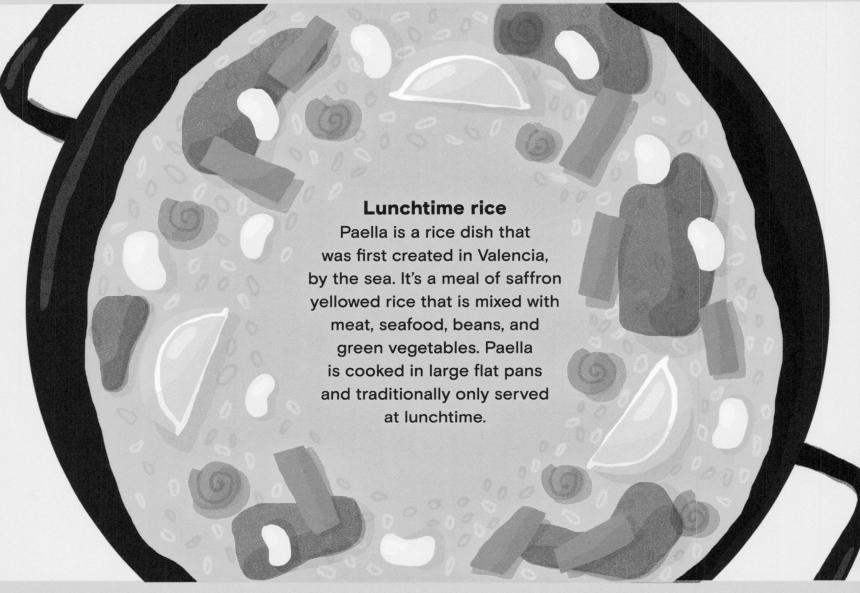

Lunchtime rice

Paella is a rice dish that was first created in Valencia, by the sea. It's a meal of saffron yellowed rice that is mixed with meat, seafood, beans, and green vegetables. Paella is cooked in large flat pans and traditionally only served at lunchtime.

Tapas

Tapas are small dishes. Some are warm, others are cold. Tapas are a great way to eat many different kinds of food at one meal. Tapa means "cover" or "lid." The term originally came from the slices of meat and bread drinkers used to cover their glasses to keep flies away.

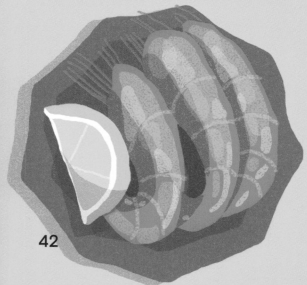
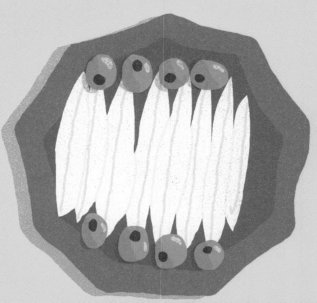

42

In Spain, on the evening of January 5, children leave their shoes outside at night because the next day is Día de los Reyes!

DÍA DE LOS REYES
Three Kings' Day

In the morning, the children wake to find their shoes filled with gifts. Then breakfast is a cake covered in candied fruits, which is called a roscón de reyes. Baked inside the cake, there is one small prize wrapped in paper and one bean. Whoever finds the prize is said to be royalty for the day. Whoever finds the bean has to pay for next year's cake!

GERMANY

The land of the sausage

In Germany, there are more than 1,500 types of sausage, including bockwurst, leberwurst, knackwurst, landjäger, blutwurst, and bratwurst. Sausages come in all shapes, sizes, and flavors. They are eaten in buns or on their own for breakfast, lunch, and dinner. A sausage can even be cut up and sprinkled on top of soup.

Baking

A pretzel is a special bread famous for its shape. First the soft dough is shaped into a knot. Then it is baked until shiny and brown, and topped with salt. A pretzel is said to bring good luck. Some people think a pretzel looks like hands in prayer.

WEIHNACHTEN
Christmas

The tradition of putting up an evergreen tree for Christmas started in Northern Europe around 1,000 years ago. Then, in the nineteenth century in Germany, people put trees up inside their homes. The trees were decorated with candles, nuts, apples, and pretzels. This tradition was taken up by Queen Victoria and her family in England. Soon it became a popular custom in many countries.

The beginning of the Christmas season starts at the end of November with Advent. At this time of year many German towns hold big Christmas markets, with stalls selling hot drinks and food. There's plenty of music, and sparkling Christmas trees too.

At Christmas there is a big meal with either roast goose and cabbage, potato salad and sausages, or poached fish.

UNITED KINGDOM

There are four countries in the United Kingdom—England, Scotland, Wales, and Northern Ireland. Different regions have their own special dishes. Many dishes are shared too.

Haggis

The national dish of Scotland is haggis, which is sheep's innards boiled inside a sheep's stomach.

Fish and chips

There are different stories about who made fish and chips first, but we do know it's been a British favorite since the 1800s.

The humble sandwich

The sandwich was named after an English aristocrat, the Earl of Sandwich. The Earl was a passionate gambler who wanted to eat food that would keep his hands clean while he played cards. He asked for meat to be put between two slices of bread, and the sandwich was born.

GUY FAWKES NIGHT

"Remember, remember the fifth of November, The Gunpowder Treason and Plot!" This old rhyme is about what happened on November 5, 1605. Guy Fawkes and a small group of plotters planned to blow up the Houses of Parliament in London, but they were discovered and stopped just in time!

Over the years a celebration called Guy Fawkes Night, or Bonfire Night, grew to mark the failed plot. Across towns, and cities bonfires are lit and there are big firework displays. In November, it is cold outside, so people bundle up warm and feast on soups, stews, hot chocolate, and toffee apples.

To this day, every November 5, guards search the parliament buildings to check for plotters.

NORTH AMERICA

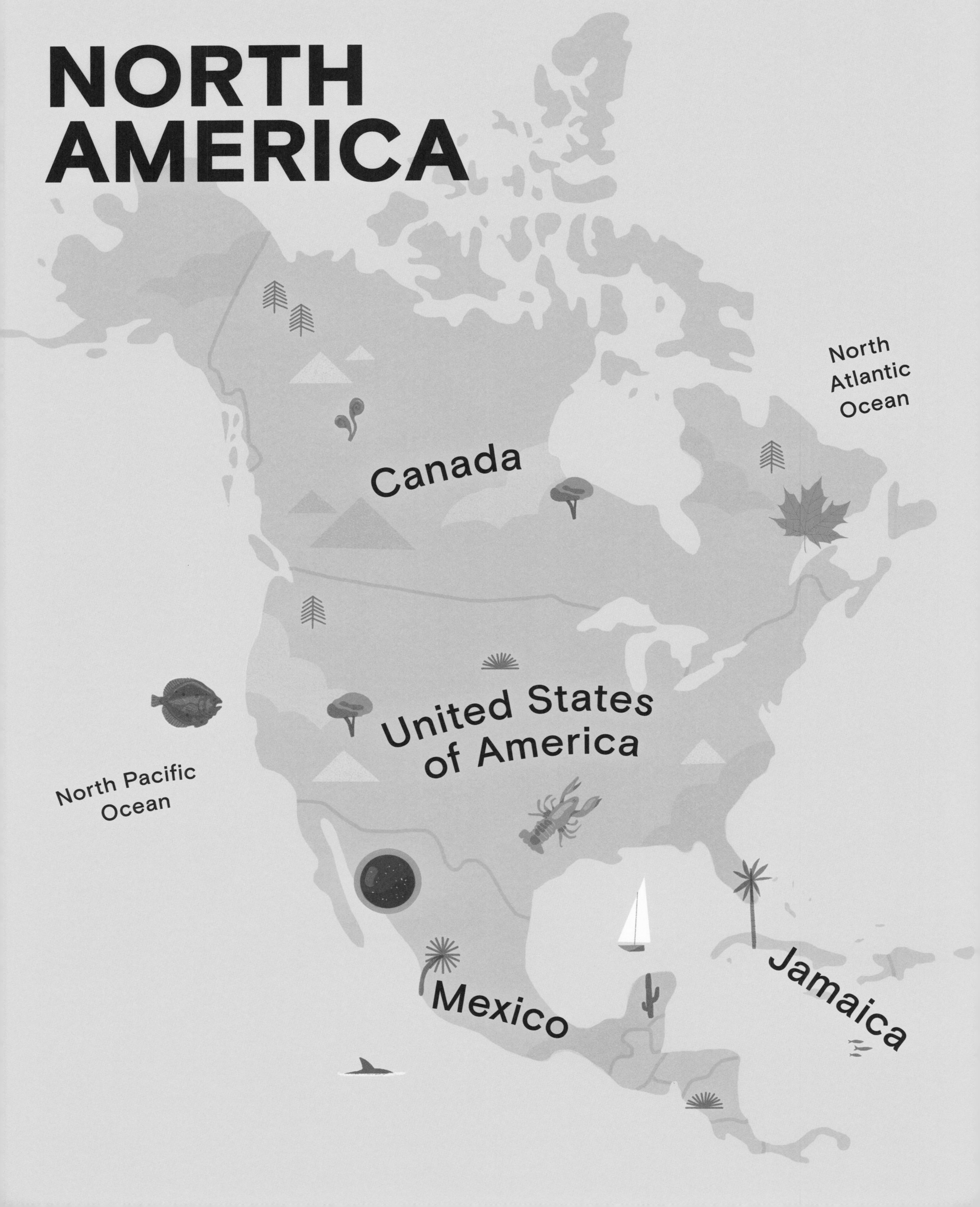

South Atlantic Ocean

South Pacific Ocean

Argentina

SOUTH AMERICA

Cacao has been eaten by people for thousands of years. The Ancient Aztecs of central Mexico roasted cacao beans, then ground them into a paste mixed with water, vanilla, chili peppers, and more spices. The drink tasted bitter compared with the hot chocolate we drink nowadays.

CHOCOLATE

In 1847, a British chocolate company, called J.S. Fry & Sons, created the first solid edible chocolate bar. Today chocolate is eaten as a treat and at celebrations all around the world. It's a great gift too.

In 1615, when the Spanish princess, Anne of Austria married the French king Louis XIII, the queen brought her love of chocolate to France. It was a luxury and only the wealthiest of lips could afford to sip small cups.

How is chocolate made?

Chocolate tastes delicious but it's difficult to make. Chocolate comes from the fruit of the cacao tree. The seed of the fruit is a large bean surrounded by a sweet white pulp in a big pod.

1. Ferment: First the sticky beans are piled in boxes, then left to ferment, or brew, for up to one week.

2. Dry: Then the beans are put out in the sun to dry.

3. Winnow: The dried beans are cracked open. A small piece, called a nib, is taken out of each bean.

4. Roast: The nibs are roasted in special ovens.

5. Grind: The roasted nibs are then ground in stone mills, making a thick paste. Most chocolate is made in this way.

MEXICO

Mexican food is fresh, colorful, and full of amazing flavors. The main flavor in most dishes comes from the use of chili peppers.

hot chili

Chili peppers

Mexico grows 150 different types of chilies, which come in all kinds of strengths and flavors, from the extremely hot to the gentle and mild. Some taste sweet and others are smoky.

Mole

The word mole comes from the Aztec "molli", which means "sauce." There are hundreds of varieties of mole.

Beans

Around 200 different kinds of beans grow in Mexico. They come in different colors, shapes, and flavors.

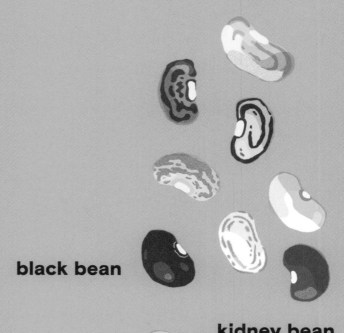

black bean

kidney bean

pinto bean

Corn

Over 59 different types of corn grow in Mexico. Masa is a dough made from corn flour. It is used in many dishes, including tortillas, which are like pancakes, and tamales, which are stuffed wraps.

DÍA DE LOS MUERTOS
Day of the Dead

The Day of the Dead is based on an ancient Aztec custom. It is held on November 1 and 2. The celebration is similar to a family reunion, except the guests of honor are family members who have passed away. It is a joyful time when loved ones are remembered. First an altar is set up at home with candles to help spirits find their way back. The altar includes some of the dead person's possessions that were important to them, as well as some of their favorite foods.

Then families head to the graveyard for a big party, with a huge feast to eat. They clean the gravestones, sing, and chat.

Pan de muerto
This is a special kind of sweetened bread. Often it is decorated with cuttings of dough shaped like bones, or baked to look like a skull.

JAMAICA

Jamaica is an island bathed in sunshine. Fruits, such as mango, pineapple, papaya, banana, guava, coconut, ackee, and plantain, grow well in its tropical climate.

Sugar cane

Most sugar is made from sugar cane juice. Raw sugar cane is peeled and eaten as a sweet snack. It can also be crushed and made into a tasty drink.

National fruit

Ackee is a bright red tropical fruit. When it's ripe, it bursts open. Inside, there is a soft, creamy yellow flesh, which is the only edible part. If an ackee is opened before it is ripe, it releases a poisonous gas.

Ackee and saltfish

This is Jamaica's national dish. Dried saltefish is soaked in water and then cooked with ackee and aromatics. It is eaten for breakfast or dinner.

54

INDEPENDENCE DAY

On August 6, Jamaicans celebrate gaining their independence from Great Britain in 1962.

/
sugar cane

During the festivities, Jamaicans celebrate their culture and cuisine. There's dancing in the streets. Street vendors sell delicious dishes prepared using the Caribbean harvest. And artists put on exhibitions of their paintings too.

Jerk chicken
"Jerking" is the Jamaican way of using spicy seasoning on food and slowly cooking it over fire. Jerk chicken is marinated in spices then grilled.

55

ARGENTINA

Argentina is a country full of vast plains called pampas. Here, there are large cattle ranches, where cowboys, or gauchos, tend to herds of roaming cattle. Argentinian beef is world famous.

Argentine dancing
Many Argentines go to dance classes to learn the tango, which is difficult to master.

Food on the go
Empanadas are little pies stuffed with beef, cheese, or vegetables. People eat them as takeout snacks and children take them to school for lunch.

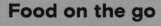

DÍA DE LA TRADICIÓN
Tradition Day

Día de la Tradición celebrates the birth of José Hernández, who was a poet who wrote about the life of the gaucho. The day is celebrated with lots of music and dancing and a great feast known as an asado.

"Asado" is the Argentinean word for "barbecue." Meat is cooked on a spit or over a big grill, which is called a "parrilla". There's plenty of food to go round. It is a time for friends and family to eat together.

UNITED STATES OF AMERICA

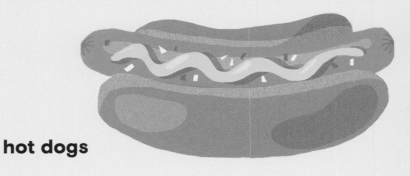

hot dogs

The United States of America, or the USA, covers a huge amount of land. From state to state, there are very different styles of food, including fried chicken and cornbread in the Deep South, grilled steak in the Midwest, and there's plenty of fresh seafood in Florida, which is surrounded by water.

taco

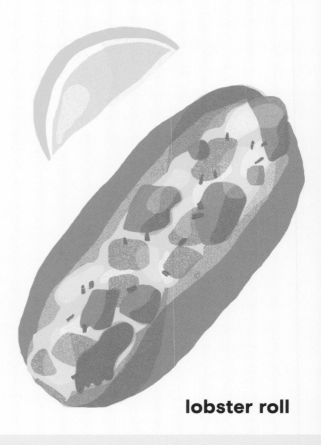

lobster roll

For thousands of years, across the world street food has been a quick and easy way to eat out and about. Meanwhile, the USA has perfected takeout.

Bagels are bread rolls in the shape of a ring! The basic roll-with-a-hole design is hundreds of years old and originated in the Jewish communities of Poland. Popular all over North America, the New York bagel is considered one of the best in the world and it is made by boiling it in water before baking it.

hamburger

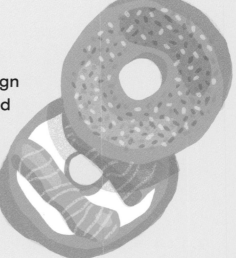

bagel

THANKSGIVING

Thanksgiving in the USA is a time to gather together with loved ones and cook and eat together, while being grateful for all that you have. It is celebrated every year on the fourth Thursday of November.

Thanksgiving has its origins in autumn harvest festivals, when people celebrated and gave thanks for a bountiful harvest that made sure they had lots of tasty food for the winter months.

Today it is still a time to say thanks, and cooking a big meal is a great way to do that. Turkey, potatoes, and pumpkin pie are just a few of the delicious foods usually eaten.

CANADA

Canada is a vast country in the far north of North America. Here, there are long harsh winters, but it is still possible to grow delicious foods.

poutine

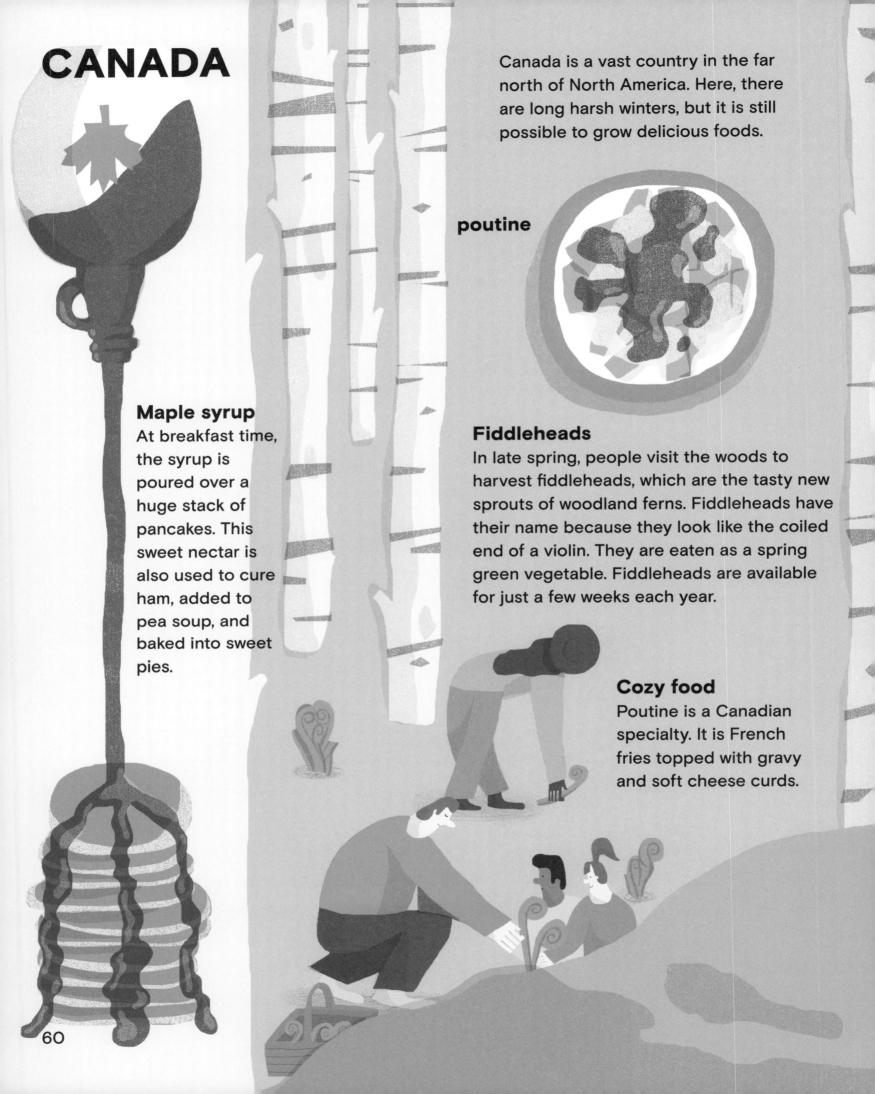

Maple syrup
At breakfast time, the syrup is poured over a huge stack of pancakes. This sweet nectar is also used to cure ham, added to pea soup, and baked into sweet pies.

Fiddleheads
In late spring, people visit the woods to harvest fiddleheads, which are the tasty new sprouts of woodland ferns. Fiddleheads have their name because they look like the coiled end of a violin. They are eaten as a spring green vegetable. Fiddleheads are available for just a few weeks each year.

Cozy food
Poutine is a Canadian specialty. It is French fries topped with gravy and soft cheese curds.

MAPLE SYRUP HARVEST

The maple leaf is a symbol of Canada. Maple syrup is the sweet sap of the maple tree. Every spring, when the weather begins to warm, the sap flows from the maple tree.

First the maple tree is drilled into, then a tap is pushed inside to collect the sap. The sap is boiled down to a sticky sweet syrup. It takes over 40 liters of maple sap to produce one liter of syrup!

Maple taffy is a type of candy made by boiling maple sap for a little longer than it would take to make syrup. The soft liquid syrup is placed in the snow to harden.

Australia

Indian Ocean

AUSTRALASIA
& OCEANIA

Pacific

Ocean

Tasman Sea

AUSTRALIA

Australia is both a country and a continent. This means that is has a unique ecosystem—some of the food grown there is not found anywhere else in the world.

Bush food

Bush tucker, or bush food, is food that is native to Australia. Aboriginal Australians have lived in Australia for over 60,000 years and know exactly what they can hunt and gather from the land to have a healthy diet. Many of these ancient foods are still widely eaten today. Bush animals such as kangaroo, emu, snake, and lizard are hunted and cooked on fires made in holes, which are covered in hot coals.

Sweet treats

Aboriginal women gather honey ants from nests found under mulga trees. The nests may be as deep as two meters underground, so it takes a lot of digging to get a handful of ants! The ants store honey in their abdomens, and the honey

can be sucked from them as a sweet treat.

CHRISTMAS

In Australia, Christmas is celebrated on December 25, which falls in the middle of summer. Children have their summer holidays from mid-December to early February, so some people might even be camping at Christmas.

Most families try to be together for Christmas, and the main meal is normally eaten at lunchtime. It is common to have a cold Christmas dinner, or a barbecue with seafood such as prawns and lobsters, along with the "traditional English" food.

Across the world, there are many different customs and ways to eat. There are different tools for eating too.

How to eat with your hands

1. First wash your hands thoroughly.
2. Use only your right hand. Mix the food with your fingertips.
3. Push a small lump of food together into a ball shape.
4. Use your last three fingers to scoop. Your thumb helps to push the food into your mouth.

LET'S EAT

How to use chopsticks

1. Hold out your hand as if you are about to shake someone's hand.

2. Tuck one chopstick under your thumb.

3. Hold the second chopstick with your pointing finger and thumb.

4. Bend your fingers. Tuck your pinkie and ring fingers up, under the lower chopstick.

5. Put your middle finger under the top stick to lever.

6. Move the top stick up and down to grab the food.

There are different ways of holding a knife and fork.

The continental way: Hold the knife and fork in different hands to cut and then eat.

The American way: The fork zigzags from one hand to the other. While cutting the food, hold the fork in one hand. Then hold it in the other hand to scoop the food into your mouth.

North America

Europe

Central America

South America

Can you spot where some
of these foods are found all
over the world?

- Soya bean
- Wheat
- Sugar cane
- Chocolate (cacao)
- Crayfish
- Rice
- Cinnamon

Asia

Middle
East

Africa

Australasia
& Oceania

THE WORLD

GLOSSARY

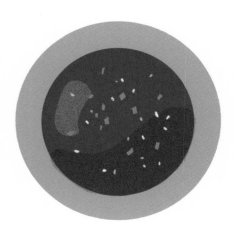

Sumac – a flowering plant, which can be dried and powdered, to be used as a spice in middle eastern cooking.

Mole – (pronounced in two syllables, moe-leh) is a classic Mexican sauce. It exists in countless versions throughout the country, varying in color, consistency, ingredients and use according to geographical location, family tradition, and local preference. It can contain as many as 30 ingredients.

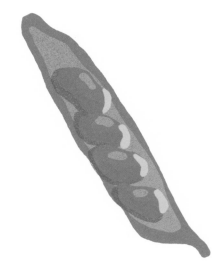

Pomegranate – a round fruit with sweet edible seeds, which is used to add both sweet and sour flavors to dishes.

Fava beans – big green beans that grow in long pods and are popular in many Mediterranean and Middle Eastern cuisines. Fava beans are almost always removed from the pods before preparing them.

Dynasty – means rulers of the same family who rule for generations to come. It also means an era during which that family ruled.

Kola nut – the seed of the cola tree, which contains caffeine and is chewed or made into a drink.

Durum wheat – a kind of hard wheat grown in dry areas, which is ground into the flour that is most commonly used to make pasta.

Barbeque or BBQ – a meal or gathering at which meat, fish, or other food is cooked outdoors on a rack over an open fire or on a special grill.

Gaucho – is a skilled horseman, with a reputation of being brave and unruly. Gauchos became greatly admired in stories and have become an important part of the cultural tradition of some South American countries.

Toffee apples – also known as candy apples in North America, are whole apples covered in a hard toffee or sugar candy coating, with a stick inserted as a handle.

Sugar cane – a tropical grass with tall, stout, jointed stems from which sugar is extracted.

Soybean or Soya Bean – a species of plant native to East Asia, widely grown for its edible bean, which has numerous uses.

Turkish delight – a sticky gelatinous sweet traditionally made of syrup and cornflour, dusted with icing sugar and most commonly flavored with rosewater.

Cumin – the dried seed of the Cuminum cyminum plant. It has been used as a spice for thousands of years and has a rich, sometimes spicy flavor.

Crayfish – a nocturnal crustacean that looks a bit like a small lobster and lives in streams and rivers.

Saffron – the spice originates from a flower called crocus sativus—commonly known as the "saffron crocus."

Cacao – are the seeds from a small tropical American evergreen tree, from which cocoa, cocoa butter, and chocolate are made.

Cinnamon – a spice obtained from the inner bark of the Cinnamon evergreen tree. This is then dried and sold as cinnamon strips that curl into rolls and can be ground into a powder.

Cured meats – curing is a way of keeping foods such as meat, fish and vegetables from going bad, by the addition of salt with the aim of drawing moisture out of the food. It also adds flavour to the food.

Ramadan – the ninth month of the Muslim year, during which fasting is observed from dawn to sunset.

Rice – the seed of the grass species Oryza sativa (Asian rice) or Oryza glaberrima (African rice).

Tubers – are vegetables which grow underground on the root of a plant.